SCOWL

REVOLUTION POEMS

Crow Hollow Books

SCOWL

Revolution Poems

JAY SIZEMORE

Published by Crow Hollow Books
Nashville, TN 37207

Manufactured print on demand.

10 9 8 7 666 5 4 3 2 1

ISBN: 978-0692522684

For the haters.

TABLE OF CONTENTS

I.

SCOWL
~after Allen Ginsberg, for Sarah

1.
I've seen the best minds of my generation
destroyed by narcissism, believing
their own hype,
that they could rewrite history on a social
media feed, standing on their armchairs with
eyes rolled back to the whites, sharks
gnashing at invisible meat in the white
sea foam,
        teeth chipped and cracking from
        clacking bone against bone,
who understood that feminists don't
swallow come, they peel back the layers
of skin from the hard cock, like dissecting a
flexed muscle, using dull tools like
fingernails buffed to an acrylic shine, no
anesthetic applied, find every fibrous layer
of meat
        and snip snip snip
who tore pages from the Vagina
Monologues and stuffed them into their
vaginas,
        ingesting false gods into the real god,
        the birth hole of Christ,
who reclaimed Anne Sexton from the
narcoleptics,

only to fuck her corpse more quietly
in the tool shed, using male tears for
lubrication of every opening,
who shouted TRIGGER WARNING from
every window of every church in the city,
any time a thought entered the mind
TRIGGER WARNING: anal sex, a fist
covered with shit, rectum flotsam and
jetsam,
TRIGGER WARNING: another woman
turning herself into a come dumpster,
a slave to the lustful male gaze,
breast implants and rouge,
TRIGGER WARNING: another cis-
gendered white man thinking about fucking
you,
TRIGGER WARNING: the leaves are
turning bright red in the fields, burning
like an empire at the end of its reign,
burning like menstruation,
Christian Grey with a bloody tampon
between his teeth,
who dismantled the patriarchy with a pair of
pliers and a blowtorch, an email inbox
stuffed with slimy testicular secrets
and empty scrotal sacks,
who made themselves invisible and made
every man a rapist in a bathroom stall,
standing in solidarity with the wind,
the wagging tongues of dogs,
redacted, redacted, redacted

2

who wrote petitions to have women stop
eating themselves, to stop the search
       for the perfect wife, the ballerina
       dancing on the head
       of Charles Bukowski's prick,
who wrote petitions and blogs and Tweets
and petitions about problematic
appropriations,
       the systemic oppression of not
       having a seat at every table,
who said Jay Sizemore is a piece of shit, Jay
Sizemore is a fucking troll, I've blocked him
       on all social media for thinking he's
       a victim,
who got a teacher fired for reading a
Ginsberg poem to the class, for daring to
       allow a poet's words to occupy his
       mouth longer than the taste of his
       lover's come,
who wore a mattress around their neck for
performance art, carrying the weight of
       a rolling stone, of an abortion scar,
       of a sex tape gone wrong,
the world is a condom kept past its
expiration date, the wrapper creased with
white wrinkles,
a Dear John letter torn to pieces
and meticulously recrafted
with Scotch tape and tears,
the world is a liar, half-drunk, urging you
into the alley with the barrel of a pistol

wedged at the bottom of your spine, the
world is a garbage truck for dreams,
removing couches from curbs, black bags
stuffed with loose foliage
from tree trimming,
the world is a dog food factory with an
undisclosed source of meat,
who said, you can be anything you want to
be if you just never give up,
                until cancer became the number one
                killer and Charles Manson died
                of a broken heart,
who built the MFA factories of the damned,
churning out carbon copy creatives
                with hatred for articles and a keen
                love of the ampersand,
who said a prostitute should be called a sex
worker and never a hooker without a sense
of humor,
                never a come guzzling whore
                working her way through college,
who requested the vampires to sparkle, for
lead female characters to only crave
attention from
                cruel, callous men, a sexual tension
                building to a broken bed,
who protested the syllabus for its inclusion
of Ovid and tales of Greek mythology
                for their content, the triggering post
                traumatic stress of fictional god rape,

4

who was offended by comedians, driving
them away from their campuses
      with pitchforks and flames, threats of
      litigation, thrown beer bottles
      to the stage,
who counts the gender of every writer in
every magazine, counts the gender
      of every editor, counts the gender of
      every facebook like, counts the
      gender of every bookstore owner,
      counts the gender of every
      cat on the lap,
who asked the world to stop reading men, to
#killallmen, to lift the skirts
      of every pixelated page and check
      for smooth plastic parts,
the new rainbow is sterile shades of gray,
every person lives in their own segregated
digital box or cell,
every person the warm nucleus at the center
of their solipsistic self,
the cluster of stars at the beginning of the
universe, around which it all revolves,
the zero model in the first line of
impressionist clones
where political correctness is the low-
hanging fruit, the bulbs of overripe outrage
dangling like exposed testicles,
the plague of man-spreading subway riders
taking up extra seats,

5

the epidemic of non-empathic man-splainers
with affinities for actually's.
who said Sansa Stark should never have
been raped, that it was time to boycott HBO,
        that George R. R. Martin should be
        castrated with a letter opener,
who rage quit the Academy Awards, the Pen
American Awards, the Grammy Awards,
        too many kids on the playground
        trying to climb on one swing set,
who watched Michael Brown get shot in the
        back, watched Eric Garner get
        choked to death,watched Tamir Rice
        lose his life in two seconds, Walter
        Scott shot unarmed,
who makes tragedy about themselves rather
than the tragic,
        putting picket lines around funerals,
        shouting God Hates Fags,
who put a glass dome over the North
American continent,
        waiting for the cannibals to come out
        of the closets,
the hunger pangs manifest like concrete
blocks thrown off rooftops,
the sun is unmerciful with its lunacy,
each room needs an oscillating fan, rattling
with white streamers,
the streets become Dutch ovens with
sky for lid,

brains boil like cabbages, making thoughts
dark with a dismal stench,
churches are slaughterhouses and prayers
are self-flagellations,
the beds are devouring the dreamers, but the
dreamers never know it.
who decided what words should never be
said, offended by the word cunt,

> with cunts capable of being used like
> Chinese finger cuffs,
> cunts used like pencil sharpeners,
> grinding dicks into hamburger,
> shitting blood all over the pages of
> the Constitution,

check your privilege,
who was offended by the word nigger,
calling for *Huckleberry Finn* to be banned,

> calling for *Tom Sawyer* to be
> eradicated from the classroom,
> as if the past were a curtain to be
> drawn, as if nigger isn't shouted
> every other word in every other pop
> song on the radio,

check your privilege,
who was offended by the picture of the
prophet Muhammad

> and shot up the printers,
> who said the artists deserve what
> they got, that action creates
> consequence,

that stirring a hornet's nest is the best
way to be stung,
check your privilege,
who was offended by *Gone With The Wind*
in a Twitter feed, filed a petition
to ruin a career, starting with one
position of influence,
and then protesting at every
scheduled performance until there is
no safe place
for poetry or art at the edges,
check your privilege,
who was offended by the word
motherfucker, and demanded an R rating,
counting the number of fucks within
every two hour span,
going home and fucking the Bible
like a dildo shaped from Jesus' head,
who was offended by gay sex, by the male
genitalia, by anything other than missionary,
wanting to protect the children from
escalating teen pregnancy
by making sexual identity and
sexual freedom a mark of shame,
overthrowing the Supreme Court to
protect the idea of selling women
for two goats and a plot of land,
waving the Confederate flag,
who was offended by lack of Christian faith,
forcing candidates to say they love God,

the word atheist like a dirty sock in
the mouth,
religion that opiate the drunk mob
force feeds like fire
to their children made
of cutout paper,
who was offended by Jared Leto playing a
transgendered male on film,
wanting all actors to stop acting and
start only playing themselves,
check your privilege,
who was offended by a rape joke, offended
by a duckface, offended by a blowjob,
offended by a staggering lack of
privacy, with all emails made public,
offended by another man fetishizing
the female body,
offended by rape drug-detecting nail
polish,
offended by any singular comment
that strikes a bad chord,
offended by the notion of equality of
opportunity trumping equality of
outcome,
offended by Caitlyn Jenner being
called a hero,
offended by Caitlyn Jenner having
more money than most identity-
struggling teens,
offended by the Nobel Prize,
offended by Coca-Cola forgetting

your name,
offended by anything that exists
outside the solipsistic self,
who observes such freedom of expression
with an indignant scowl,
anamorphic time travelers, clothed in
Puritan rags,
scowling from the wilderness before
it was named,
scowling from the pulpit of haloed
light,
scowling from the mirror and the
stranger's face,
who can't breathe amid all this strangulation
of ideas, this tightening lynch knot
around the throat of the free, the
burdensome gaggle of lampreys
clinging to the body of the immortal
giant, the leeches feeding
on the blood of their own making, a
new form of vampiric anorexia,
the streets are gorged with this silent war,
hands turned into lenses, eyes
turned into mirrors,
all windows are LCD screens, the skyline is
a flickering continuum of YouTube
viral video,
we are running out of drinking water,
reservoirs turning yellow as urine, nothing
but bleached sand,

the California forests are a tinderbox, a
funeral pyre for man,
while PornHub raises money to see people
fuck in outer space, to see semen float in
zero gravity,
while elephants are getting their heads
blown apart,
the white rhino has seen its last days,
half the world living in denial of man-made
climate change,
vilifying the homeless taking baths in public
restroom sinks,
ignoring the scent of car exhaust cloaked
alleys, of unlaundered
sweat-stained fatigues,
of sewer steam drifting ripe through rusted
grate, of garbage left untilled in a landfill,
ignoring the taste of the spoiled, rancid
meat, the rotted fruit clouded with flies,
the salt in a lover's sweat, the last cup of
coffee ever served,
the future is a butchery,
the tabletops run with the blood of the poets,
tongueless mouths open and gargling a
strangled yawp,
splattering droplets of crimson rain,
no words are sacrosanct,
no bone is immune to the hammer and saw,
who will stand in front of the armored tank,
placing a daisy in the cannon's black maw,

who will join hands in a circle that becomes
a net, a mesh of forgiveness
cushioning the fall of humanity, and saving
our truest selves,
the meteor of guilt caught like
a bird in a cage,
taught to fly and hunt only for worms,
instead of feasting on the carrion of decay,
the unbalanced wheel of life resuming its
perfect spin,
with every voice taking part in that
harmonious song.

2.

Reflections aren't capable of cracking
skulls, aren't capable of pinning tongues to
the roofs of mouths, of painting windows
shut, sealing doors with hammered nails.
Hail Satan! The deceiver. The Morning Star.
The white man.

      Nightmare made flesh, made lover,
      made king of everything on Earth.
Hail Satan! The torture device! The wireless
router! The justice system!

      Satan, whose year-end bonus is the
      world's salaries combined,
      Satan, whose wristwatch is made of
      human kidneys,
      Satan, who put a padlock on the
      clitoris and declared rape children
      miracles.
Hail Satan! The cellular phone! The dick-
pic! The Saudi Arabian prince!

      Satan, who invented the
      high-heeled shoe.
      Satan, who invented fast food!
      Satan, who started the Industrial
      Revolution with steam.
Hail Satan! The pharmaceutical giant! The
income gap! The minimum wage!

      Satan, who enslaved the world to the
      concept of ownership.
      Satan, who made addicts to
      happiness, who made sadness a sin.

        Satan, who invented the concept of
        race.
Hail Satan! The holocaust! The red
wedding! The abortion clinic!
        Satan, porn industry mogul, shrimp
        boat captain, the new Pope.
        Satan, who refuses to free the nipple!
        Satan, who condemns assisted
        suicide!
Hail Satan! Member of the Academy!
Congressional lobbyist! Child molester!
        Satan, who teaches creationism in
        the classroom.
        Satan, who builds the bombs.
        Satan, the river of time.
Hail Satan! His cliched red horns! The
mustache! The American Native!
        Satan, who murdered the buffalo for
        their tongues.
        Satan, who forced Chinese feet into a
        golden lotus.
        Satan, who built the railroad.
Hail Satan! The Masque of the Red Death!
The Raven! The Hellbound Heart!
        Satan, who clips the birds wings.
        Satan, who sets the emission
        standard.
        Satan, the military recruiter who
        wanders the halls of high schools.
Hail Satan! OPEC! Warmonger! President
of the United States!

14

Satan, whose furnace is
fed with coal.
Satan, whose teeth shine slick with
human fat.
Satan, who turns the Grand Canyon
into a mall.
Hail Satan! MLB! NFL! NBA!
Satan, reinventing the slave with a
leather bound ball.
Satan, claiming ownership of the
sun.
Satan, charging a fee to breathe.
Hail Satan! King of the coral reef! Toxic
waste dump! Graveyard tyrant!
Satan, who arms the rebels.
Satan, who trains jihadis to fly.
Satan, owner of Fox News.
Hail Satan! The police state! The
carpetbagger! The candidate!
Satan, who bailed out the banks.
Satan, who killed the electric car.
Satan, the blindness of human palms.
Satan who stands on the backs of the
divided, cracking his whip, breaking the
bodies made of water, captain of the slave
ship carried by multitudes of hummingbirds
strung to the sails,
floating above everything, so that people are
no more significant than ants,
but when the giants fall, it's the ants that eat
the bodies.

3.
I'm with you, Sarah,
in your bedroom when your daddy knocks
on the door.
I'm with you, Sarah,
when you wake up naked on the floor.
I'm with you, Sarah,
when the world starts to spin like an out of
control ferris wheel.
I'm with you, Sarah,
when he says you can trust him, when he
lets you leave a toothbrush at his place,
when he makes you late for work with
another blackmail blowjob,
I'm with you, Sarah,
when you have to flip the mattress to hide
the blood,
I'm with you, Sarah,
in New York City, where you got those
bruises on your arms,
like purple handcuffs, like clumsy
tiger stripes,
I'm with you, Sarah,
when you wash your hands for the
hundredth time a day,
when lotion burns in the cracks of your skin,
I'm with you, Sarah,
when you post another selfie, asking for
faceless approval,
I'm with you, Sarah,

when you touch yourself and imagine being
raped, being dominated
by a force too powerful to feel
anything but lust,
I'm with you, Sarah,
when you cry yourself to sleep,
when you smother your screams into the
cotton pillowcase,
I'm with you, Sarah,
when you feel like it's you
against the world,
when no one believes your story,
when the police officer looks at you like
you asked for it,
when the layers of your clothing still leave
you shivering underneath,
I'm with you, Sarah,
and I know you are strong enough to make it
on your own,
but I'll put my arm around your shoulders
if you're ever tired of feeling alone.

II.

Three minutes 'til midnight

It's three minutes 'til midnight
and most of the world has stopped
wearing a watch, getting YOLO
tattooed across their wrists.

The ocean told me what Jesus'
feet felt like, in a whisper
from a seashell ceasing
to reflect rainbows.

Jesus is the name of every atomic bomb.
Jesus is the face in the mushroom cloud.
Jesus is the ash of civilizations.
Jesus is SPF one trillion:
won't wash off in baptism.

It's three minutes 'til midnight
and soon will be two.
The shapes in the waves
will be the exposed bellies
of multitudes forgetting how to swim,
shining and swollen
in an unforgiving sun.

Jesus is coming back,
my grandmother told me,
my mother told me,
Paul told me
in stories

I could not bear to believe
shoveling dirt onto coffin lids.

There's a smell of pungent decay
seeping up through my skin,
an odor that cannot be cleansed
except through flame,
the stench of a beached whale
opening its eyes
and thrashing through a yawning mouth
disguised as a prayer.

Jesus is not coming back,
he's been here for ages,
inside the carburetor
of every engine that revs,
every engine that hums
thighs into a tingling trance
on those long commutes
to and from Hell.
Jesus is an erection made of steel.

It's three minutes 'til midnight,
and soon it will be just one,
seconds counting down
like shallow breaths under a sheet.
Our children can't tell time
and their savior

is the slow suicide
of cigarette smoke

and ultraviolet light,
a Corvette Christ
driven into the sun.

THIS POEM IS A PICTURE OF THE PROPHET MUHAMMAD
~for Charlie Hebdo

This poem is the prophet Muhammad
fucked by a ribs-thin mule.
This poem is the prophet Muhammad
sucking Jesus Christ's cock.
This poem is the prophet Muhammad
licking the asshole of a pig.

This poem is the prophet Muhammad
pouring gasoline on the Quran
while Jewish rabbis tickle his
feet with feathers.
This poem is the prophet Muhammad
turned into a slave
crushing pigments into powder
for the paint artists will use
to render blasphemies so beautiful
even the prophet Muhammad must smile.

This poem is a woman
raping the prophet Muhammad
with a chair leg wrapped in barbed wire,
acid-faced ghosts
pressing his body to the dirt,
seventy virgins gathered like crows
to point and laugh
and throw rocks at god.
This poem is the prophet Muhammad

made servant to Buddha and Shiva,
feeding them grapes by hand
while they masturbate with the Black Stone.

This poem is the prophet Muhammad
kissing the American flag.
This poem is the prophet Muhammad
bowing to worship the golden calf.
This poem is the prophet Muhammad
with his pants pulled down
showing the world his vagina.

TAYLOR SWIFT CAN'T TRADEMARK MY TONGUE

I give my sick beat antibiotics and aspirin.
I give my sick beat vitamin C.
The worst thing is when a beat vomits
in your car, rattles the rearview mirror,
makes your head feel like a cavern
turned into a conga drum.
I keep my beat healthy
to avoid the ear worms.

I can't party like it's 1989,
all of my parties took place post 1990.
The years before, I was a tumbleweed,
blown through changes
the way reflections stream past
on the outsides of car windows.
I was as popular as mathematics.
My best friends were the knight and bishop.
I'm still learning how to relax.

Nice to meet you, where you been?
I've been here
waiting for you to read my poem.
My name is somewhere on this page.
Maybe you can teach me how to dance,
how to wash the scent of cat piss
out of a couch cushion,
how to put a bow around nothing
because it is all I could afford.

I could show you incredible things,
I could show you how everything is normal,
even the most beautiful sunset,
even the most violent of storms,
even that late night call
telling you your father is trying to die,
is in a helicopter flying
to find his next heartbeat,
these are just symptoms
of a world taking breaths.

We never go out of style,
except when we do.
I will be out of style tomorrow,
if I am in style today,
so keep me on the cusp of a change,
a butterfly learning to exist
inside its pupa stage.

Heaven is real(ly weird)

Today, I choked on my Mountain Dew,
and in that moment of breathlessness,
God revealed to me
the true image of heaven
through a starbursting halo of light
in the Taco Bell window.

There were men with microwaves for faces,
dragonfly wings in rows along their spines
like flightless Stegosauruses. Their hands
were made of cotton candy
and they offered them to me,
their sweet smell like stripper sweat,
a checkered luminescent hum
in place of ghostly smiles.

The clouds glittered and swirled
around my ankles and when I saw God
sitting on a giant boombox like a throne,
the atmosphere filled with music
that made no sense, harp strings
scrubbed with a power drill. The streets
were black vinyl and the angels
had cantilever feet with black diamond
heels,
stirring more music as they skated
along the grooved roads,
sapphire skyscrapers bending
like electrical currents overhead.

28

They asked me to stay,
to drink champagne from their nipples,
to chop off my testicles
and cast aside the worldly wants
of such weak animal flesh.
I could feel myself beginning to hum,
to emit light through my eyes,
to accept my place in the treble clef
of this discordant symphony,
and when I looked down
my legs had become the blades
in a pair of scissors,
each step taken,
eviscerating my manhood.

I gasped and snapped from the vision,
finding instead of Fire Sauce
a tiny translucent wing
left in my palm,
like a slip from a fortune cookie
you can only see yourself in.

Fukushima Franco: facebook poem #34

ontological beach bums recite Aesop's
fables to the thirsty crows.
dogs riding shotgun with their faces
to the wind,
believe in gun control.
a litany of blowjobs and fairy tales written
in irradiated veins.
Fukushima arrogance in
embryonic fracking,
a birthday party for sidewalks.
the bank is a beaten horse
dehydrated and sad,
Dick Cheney in a uterus.
postmodern dervish condom-vending-
machine-macabre,
storm cloud mosquitos.
black-hearted vinyl kiss for a wheelchair
parking space,
surrogate wedding cake.
religious grammar made
of bullets and spears
for domesticated ears.
Thanos is grateful for wax wings and
medical marijuana,
spider bites, fallen trees, Woody Guthrie.
lost Tupperware lids playing
folk concerts for Exxon,

an Ebola epigraph for rain.
a pluviophile manifesto written with a
butcher knife,
jabber jaw cathedral of rats.
James Franco takes credit for the ceasefire
a salesman for fly swatters.

SCIENCE BITCH, FACEBOOK POEM #23

The Hadron-Collider is a treadmill
shaking raindrops from a dog's coat.
Turn your body into a geometric shape,
a troll in the mountains.
Binge watch the ferns die.
J.K. Rowling took a stick of hickory
to a water spout, hired an elephant
to lick her postage stamps.
Yadda, yadda, yadda,
graffiti is an artist's peacock feather.
Peeling Scotch tape for the X-rays,
like a canoe paddled through
a chess board. Throw your baby
into the swimming pool.
Africa has penis envy,
which is as ironic as ironing
your facial skin
the day you pay off your student loans.
When the moon hatches
like a spider's egg sack,
we'll do the hokey-pokey
and turn ourselves into
climate change deniers.

BACK AND FORTH, FACEBOOK POEM #33

A car dealership like a drop in the milk bucket,
what if the Adam's apple was a tire swing?

Every woman has a face beneath her face,
a place where high heels and stockings don't
exist.

For some, selfies are a second language,
a way of speaking without words and gender
norms.

Do a podcast through a dirty projector,
kittens and Jack Daniels for brunch.

There's a hope to live in the white sea foam,
homeless housing modeled after birth control
pills.

Butter your toast with a violin bow,
daisies and dream homes exchanging masks.

An assassination attempt on Buddha
puts an earthquake in her crawling skin.

Netanyahu is loyal to water colors and mead,
a vagina in the wall, giving birth to an octopus.

The hive mind tree trunk wizard,
spins reds and blues into a wonderland for
crows.

WHISPERS OF THE TRUTH,
FACEBOOK POEM #31

The sliver moon's sharpened ends
are like the horns of a steer,
and a pointed finger can become
a makeshift pistol, firing scorn.

Rabbis suck the blood from
circumcised penis tips, herpes
for newborns. Rainbows only show up
after storms, near waterfalls, in parades.

Quantum mechanics cannot explain
a family's illogical love, taking a child
out of quarantine, and back to the city.
Frankenstein's bride wore no make-up.

Restricted numbers must be ignored,
much like Americans ignore genocide.
Someone's uncle is lost at sea,
they're calling off the search.

Tell me what the clouds look like there,
where old friends are getting older,
the photographs were taken before digital,
bras filled with wine and Chopin sadness.

They're calling it the Gaza Massacre,
bodies wrapped in sheets line the streets.

America takes its shoes off at the beach,
please just listen when someone else speaks.

ART MADE FROM ASHES:
A MESSAGE TO ISIS

Can you burn all the words
out of my mouth?
Can you rip the colors from the landscape,
make the horizon as pale as your palm?
Can you rub sand in the eyes of the past,
feeding photographs, and pages to the flame
stolen from a dragon's throat,
a blurred and holy reverence
for unwashed genitals?
Al-hamdu lillahi rabbil 'alamin.

Allah is a cunt.
Allah is a coward.
Allah is a rapist
of women and children,
the number one customer
of gay porn websites.
Allahu akbar.

Your legacy is the sound of dust
sifting through the detritus,
your prayers are the wind
stirring plumes of chalky dirt
amid the decay. Your god is a liar,
and a thief of joy,
a cloying scent of perfume
slathered onto a rotting corpse.
In sha' Allah, then disappear.

Murder makes a martyr of art,
and chaos is a shrine to chaos,
built on the bones of the damned,
and we are all damned,
every last one of us.
Assulamu' alaikum.

Author's Note

All of these poems but one were published by the now rebooted online literary journal Revolution John Magazine, run by Sheldon Lee Compton. My gratitude and respect to Sheldon for having the courage to publish such challenging work.

It's rather unfortunate that we live in a world that now feels justified in its narcissism of thinking it knows better than the individual what is acceptable as a form of creative expression. This new trend of intimidation through online bullying and shaming is setting a dangerous precedent for censorship through public opinion. Just like any other right, freedom of expression can be limited if the public wants it to be. The right to offend should be just as valid as the right to be offended.

The last poem in the collection was published and then retracted from an issue of Crab Fat Magazine after more pressure from the internet shame mob. Special thanks to author Christoph Paul for his support during that time. All these poems are presented here in defiance of wishes that they never be seen again by the public, as due to controversy, I have been blacklisted by many publications.

Thanks to everyone who reached out and supported me while I was in the crosshairs of this character assassination attempt. You know who you are, and your support is invaluable to my mental health. This includes my wife, who is always on my side and wanted to personally kick a lot of people's asses.

About the Author

Jay Sizemore doesn't have an MFA, an MBA, or a PHD. He sold his soul to corporate America and spends his days digging a grave the size of a shopping mall. Somehow, his written work has found its way into many online and print publications. He's never been nominated for a Pushcart Prize (like everyone else). His previous chapbooks are available on Amazon. Currently, he lives in Nashville, TN with his wife and two cats. Connect with him at jaysizemore.com.

www.ingramcontent.com/pod-product-compliance
Lightning Source LLC
Chambersburg PA
CBHW021942040426
42448CB00008B/1203